Pray Now

2010

Daily Devotions for the Year 2010

Published on behalf of the

OFFICE FOR WORSHIP AND DOCTRINE,
MISSION AND DISCIPLESHIP COUNCIL,
THE CHURCH OF SCOTLAND

SAINT ANDREW PRESS
Edinburgh

First published in 2009 by
SAINT ANDREW PRESS
121 George Street
Edinburgh EH2 4YN

ISBN 978 0 86153 393 0

British Library Cataloguing in Publication Data
A catalogue record for this book is available from the British Library

It is the publisher's policy to only use papers that are natural and recyclable and that have been manufactured from timber grown in renewable, properly managed forests. All of the manufacturing processes of the papers are expected to conform to the environmental regulations of the country of origin.

Typeset by Waverley Typesetters, Fakenham
Manufactured in Spain

Contents

Preface

The theme of journeying, literally and figuratively, recurs time and again in our Christian faith. Think of God's call to Abraham to leave his home and go to a new country and of the journey of the Israelites through the desert to the Promised Land. Think of Mary's journey to Bethlehem and of Paul's missionary journeys throughout the eastern Mediterranean. Think of the description of the Christian life as a journey or pilgrimage – 'Guide me, O thou great Jehovah, pilgrim through this barren land' as the well-known hymn expresses it.

On choosing the theme of journeys for the 2010 edition of *Pray Now*, the writers focus our thoughts and prayers on a key concept that is rich in resources for reading, reflection and prayer.

I am sure that *Pray Now 2010* will both deepen the faith and enrich the devotional life of all who use it and I warmly commend this booklet as an accompaniment to private and family prayer and devotion.

REV. ALAN D. BIRSS
Convener, The Task Group on Worship and Doctrine
of the Mission and Discipleship Council

Using this Book and CD

At the end of the Scottish Year of Homecoming, and as the church prepares to mark the 100th anniversary of the 1910 World Mission conference in Edinburgh, we have been thinking a lot about how far we have travelled as people and as a church. Whether we go to far-flung places, encounter new cultures or simply stay at home facing new challenges and experiences, all of us journey in some way. This year, the Pray Now Group have written prayers that reflect on different types of journey (emotional and physical) as well as different aspects and stages of journeying like departures, being on the road and arrivals. Of course, we all travel through life in unique ways and indeed people will journey through *Pray Now* in a way that is most beneficial to them but there is a truth that unites on the way and always brings us home – God is with us, wherever we are and whatever we encounter; we are on the journey together.

Once again, there is a CD to complement the contents of the book. The CD has six tracks, each introducing a different theme on the environment, followed by a reading of one of the daily prayers from that section in the book. You have the option of using the book consistently throughout the month and the CD from time to time, or of alternating the use of both mediums on different days depending on time available and indeed the circumstances of readers or listeners.

The 31-day format gives structure and pattern to the month for those who like to move through Day 1 to Day 31 in a natural progression. You may wish to choose a prayer from one of the six sections, using a different section each day, or you may just prefer to dip in and out of the book. Whatever is most helpful to you is recommended. We hope, however, whether you are sitting quietly in your favourite chair in the house, or at your desk at work, or listening in the car or kitchen, at home or on holiday, through using *Pray Now* reflection around the journeys we have been on – and are on – will help us to discover and understand God with us in deeper, enriching ways.

GAYLE TAYLOR
Convener of the Pray Now *Group*

Days of the Month

Arrivals

Life is a series of arrivals. Some are planned and others come upon us unexpectedly. Every arrival signifies that a journey has been made whether whole or in part. We describe the life-changing event of the birth of a child as 'a new arrival' and when our golden years arrive we say 'old age doesn't come by itself'! An arrival is irreversible – there is no going back. We cannot 'un-arrive'.

An arrival may be a new moment of possibility or an awakening. It may be the reaching of a new destination or a leaving behind or a homecoming. We may be the recipient of another's arrival in our life. Each arrival is an event – big or small.

The arrival of Jesus made incarnate the Word of God. The arrival of Judas in the garden of Gethsemane initiated the chain of events that led to the lifesaving cross of Christ. The arrival of Mary Magdalene at the empty tomb revealed the mind-blowing, presence of the Risen Christ. The arrival of Jesus on the road to Emmaus and his breaking of bread at supper taught us that Christ is made manifest in every act of hospitality. And the arrival of the Holy Spirit birthed the church and gifted us with the universal language of love.

Life is a series of arrivals .... until .... We finally arrive at the place God want us to be.

ARRIVALS

So Noah went out with his sons and his wife and his sons' wives. And every animal, every creeping thing, and every bird, everything that moves on the earth, went out of the ark by families.

~ Genesis 8:18–19 ~

Arrival
is a coming home.
A storm-tossed boat
scraping hull on rough rock;
a runaway rebel
resting at heaven's gateway;
a travel-weary king
stooping at life's threshold.
I have arrived, Lord;
recognised a refuge,
felt stone, earth and hay beneath me.

Arrival
is an awakening.
An embracer in a garden,
changing worlds with a kiss;
a hungry fisherman
surf-sliding to a stranger on a beach;
a sudden-struck blind man
straining for new light.
I have chosen, Lord,
and been chosen,
with soiled heart and solid hands.

Arrival
is a leaving behind.
A thief restored
with paradise promises;
a dawn-dulled woman
startled by a gaping grave;
a faith-fragile friend
declaring there's no doubt.
Here I go, Lord,
into the open-armed unknown,
believing in welcomes.

I may not come as a surprise, Lord,
or deserve a prodigal's banquet.
But I expect you're expecting me
just as I am.

Readings

Genesis 28:10–17	*Jacob's dream at Bethel*
Matthew 2:7–11	*The kings arrive in Bethlehem*
Mark 14:43–6	*Judas betrays Jesus*
Acts 9:1–9	*Paul's conversion*
Luke 23:39–43	*The repentant thief is promised a place in Paradise*
John 20:1, 2; 11–18	*Mary at the empty tomb*
John 20:19–28	*Thomas believes*

Prayer Activity

If you could go anywhere right now, where would it be? Picture that place in your mind. Imagine arriving there and the feelings that creates. Thank God for the place that makes you feel comfortable, refreshed, at home.

Prayer for the Church

For those involved with new and creative ministries and concerned with presenting the Christian faith in accessible ways

especially within emerging ministries taskgroup, the transformation ream and New Charge developments.

Blessing

In our going and our coming,
In our leaving and our arriving,
In the strangeness of the unknown
And the familiarity of home,
Grant us your blessing, Lord,
And bring us rejoicing to the places
Where we may recognise and welcome you.   AMEN

LET US GO TO THE HOUSE OF THE LORD

*Surely goodness and mercy shall follow me
all the days of my life,
and I shall dwell in the house of the Lord
my whole life long.*

~ Psalm 23:6 ~

God,
When our hopes fade and life is hard,
when our faith is shakey and the world uncertain,
when we feel that praying is the wrong thing to do
because we have no words, no good things to say, no way to begin …
let us journey to your house, Lord.

Your church;
place of sanctuary and peace –
the community of the forgiven,
the body of Christ,
where some have words when others have no voice,
where all are welcome and remembered.

In confident intercession we pray this day
for those weighed down by a situation in their family:
a feud, a betrayal, an argument about blame.
And we ask, God, that you would be in the midst
enabling apologies and change, restoration and wholeness.
Gentle God, we ask for your peace this day
in the lives of those who struggle without light or hope
due to overwhelming news, those coming to terms with illness,
or the loss of a loved one, and those who feel that no one understands.

God of creation, Calvary and the empty tomb,
you house those in need of protection and refuge,
you shelter those with fear and fatigue,
In your presence, with your people,
we are heard and known and loved.
We begin and return to you
for you, God, are our home.

Readings

Psalm 122   *Let us go to the house of the Lord*
Psalm 127   *Unless the Lord builds the house*

Prayer Activity

A story to reflect on …

THE LOCKED CHURCH

He walked up the path to the beautiful church. A quiet time, alone with God, a time of peace, a time to collect his thoughts. But when he reached the door and turned the handle he found the door was locked. Then he saw the piece of paper pinned to the door. *'Sorry, I'm not here. I'm out there. God.'*

Prayer for the Church

That pilgrims, travellers and visitors may journey safely, find friendship on arrival, and discover benefit and spiritual enlightenment in the process

especially from Scottish Churches' World Exchange, St Colm's International House in Edinburgh and local initiatives of hospitality.

Blessing

God,
be light for us
be warmth for those we love
be Father and future and eternal hope
through Jesus Christ our Lord.   AMEN.

DISCOVERY

When he was at the table with them, he took bread, blessed and broke it, and gave it to them. Then their eyes were opened, and they recognised him; and he vanished from their sight. They said to each other, 'Were not our hearts burning within us while he was talking to us on the road, while he was opening the scriptures to us?'

~ Luke 24:30–2 ~

It's a rough road;
the growing and grieving,
the learning and living,
the losing and the loving,
the stumbling and the saving.
Still, amidst the blessings and the blisters,
you looked for me, Lord.

There were obstacles;
the rumours and the wrongs,
the doubt and disbelief,
the scandal and the scorn,
the bile and the betrayal.
Still, when hatred hid your humanity,
you found me, Lord.

Then there was bread on the table
and wisdom in your eyes
and love on your lips.
And, in a cascade of crumbs,
blind fears and blinkered doubts
scattered before your open hands,
and you knew me, Lord.

And in that divine discovery
a lifetime of loving was let loose
and my silent, stifled soul
shouted and was set free.

I'm glad you stumbled on me
on your way to that table, Lord.
I'm glad you recognised in me

something worth the seeking.
Look out for me again,
for I yearn to hear your words
tumbling again like grain.

Readings

Genesis 18:9–12	*Sarah learns she is to have a child*
Genesis 45:25–8	*Jacob learns Joseph is still alive*
1 Samuel 16:8–13	*The anointing of David*
Luke 2:15–18	*The shepherds go to Bethlehem to see Jesus*
Matthew 17:1–9	*The transfiguration of Jesus*
John 20:26–8	*Thomas recognises Jesus*
Acts 2:1–4	*The coming of the Holy Spirit*

Prayer Activity

God often surprises us in the commonplace and ordinary things of life. When were you last surprised by God? Let your prayer today be the surprising of someone else with a sign of God's love.

Prayer for the Church

As we explore the idea of the Christian gospel as an alternative story to live by, in modern culture, and who it might shape drama, art and music amidst life

especially the Scottish Storytelling Centre and wider work of the Netherbow.

Blessing

God in our seeking and our seeing,
God in our questions and our believing,
God in the everyday and the astonishing,
God on the road and at our table,
God at our side and in our souls,
God of grace and blessing
today and forever.   AMEN.

IMMIGRATION

'Arise, walk through the length and the breadth of the land, for I will give it to you.'

~ Genesis 13:17 ~

The crazy moment when I realised I'd said yes to this
Lit a flame of possibility, which consumed
All the old negatives of my life; replaced,
With an unknown *future*,
The way I'd always presumed things would go.

That flame still burns, hope and excitement conmingled,
As I come into this newness.

Everything is new around me. *Everything*
Fills me with a new sense of life's immediacy.
For I have arrived in a moment awash with possibility,
And you, Lord, have opened this to me...

Soon, newness will yield again to the routine;
Soon this glorious, fragile, vulnerable me,
Reborn from the split chrysalis of my hardened past,
Will – necessarily – harden in the air of a new mundaneness.

Yet, Lord, graciously, from time to time
Reawaken in me the feelings of this moment
This brilliant living on the cusp of yesterday and tomorrow;
Let this moment – the *"Now!"* – of my arrival
From yesterday's holding-patterns of numb existence
Into the arrivals lounge of life in fullness,
Be the start of *who-knows-what*, with You.

Readings

Genesis 12:1–3 (compare with Mark 1:16–20)
Genesis 13:14–18
Genesis 15:8–17
Joshua 1:1–9
Psalm 18
Psalm 118:1–5
Matthew 6:25–34
Hebrews 11:1–13
Hebrews 12:18–24

Prayer Activity

Think of a notion that occasionally seizes you, or a thought that you once had that you might change your life in a radical way. (Perhaps you are in the middle of acting on such a thought anyway— if not, it doesn't matter.) Think through the new world such a move might put you in. What would be different? What would be better? Where would God be, in that new life, and new world? And, in *that* light – where is God in your life, and your world, as they are now?

Prayer for the Church

Those in my congregation who week by week seek out the stranger and offer friendship and those who welcome people to our church buildings and services

especially the work of The Well in Glasgow working with the Asian community there and congregations who welcome and engage with immigrants and asylum seekers as they try to embrace a new culture. The Church's Inter-faith worker.

Blessing

Let us rejoice
That today and tomorrow and tomorrow
Are in God's hands.
Let us be bold,
And claim his promises.
For God has brought us here
And Christ goes before us
And his Spirit guides us where we go.

LIFESTAGES – FROM CHILD TO ADULT

'Now I know only in part; then will I know fully, even as I have been fully known.'

~ I Corinthians 13:12 ~

You call me forth,
to play upon the stage of life;
an actor in Your great drama.
My entrance is not without struggle.
I fall and bump about the set
learning how to move with grace.
Words and sounds jumble around
until shared language connects me.
My mind broadens and quickens
as little by little the plot unfolds.
One day, I dream,
the complete works will be revealed.

But for now, I journey on –
from the spontaneity of childhood
to the teenager rebellion years
until to all intents and purposes
I appear to be grown-up.

But where are my lines?
I am still improvising from the original Script.
When will my character be fully developed?
I am still becoming my part.
Why do I miss so many cues?
I think I'm listening for that vital Word.

Author of Life, I belong in Your cast.
Help me to emerge gloriously from all my growing pains.
Risen Teacher, I am Your stagecraft student.
Enable me to use correction and praise in equal measure.
Spirit of Truth, keep directing me.
Empower me to act wisely and justly.

For I am Your child, God.
And this is Your show –
Manifesto Magnificat.

Readings

I Samuel 3:1–11   *Samuel learns to recognise the voice of God*
Mark 10:13–16   *Receiving the Kingdom of God as a child*
Luke 2:41–52   *Jesus' parents travel on while he stays to make his own journey*
I Corinthians 13:1–11   *St Paul's teaching on the gift of love*
Ephesians 4:7–16   *Growing up in our faith*

Prayer Activity

RIDDLE OF THE SPHINX

What walks on four legs in the morning, two legs at noon, and three legs in the evening? Oedipus solved the riddle, answering that a human crawls on all fours in infancy, walks upright on two legs in adulthood, and uses a cane as a third leg in old age. Yet morning, afternoon and evening follow each other daily. Are there times when you find it difficult to stand on your own two feet? How have you coped? Give thanks for those who lift you up when you are crawling and for those who give extra support when it is needed.

Prayer for the Church

For those involved in witnessing to, caring for and sharing Christian faith with children and their parents and organisations like Scripture Union and Urban Saints

especially the Children's Assembly, Sunday School, After School Club leaders and family workers within congregations, and those involved with iMPACT.

Blessing

May the blessing of incomplete knowledge,
and the promise that more is to come
keep You forever
in the power of the Spirit,
on the journey of Christ
in the love of God.

On the Road

For most people, going on a journey is an exciting, different experience. Leaving the ordinary, daily routines of life, travelling somewhere new, or other, stretches us and is good for us. 'A change is as good as a rest', as they say. However, after a while, being on the road is tiring. Keeping going, travelling alone, enduring different modes of transport, carrying baggage, not knowing where and when you will next eat, bathe or sleep – all these aspects of a journey can really take it out of us. Thank God, then, for the resting places; for the gracious, generous provision of hospitality, for the companions on the road, the new people we meet and the conversations we share – for these things show us what we have taken for granted before and remind us that wherever we may go, God goes with us.

SHARING DIALOGUE

They said to each other, 'Were not our hearts burning within us while he was talking to us on the road …?'

~ Luke 24:32 ~

Our paths were two parallel lines, same direction, never meeting,
Sad words flitting crabwise between us, keeping us together,
An endless, fruitless rehearsal of events, truisms, platitudes.
Sometimes, that's what it's like, with us…

Father, you, beyond speech
Are the goal of our speaking, as of our living;
For you are *the meaning* for which,
So blithely – or desperately – we substitute trivial meanings of our own,
Only to mourn your absence, even while you are there for us.

Christ, You are Language,
Inviting us to take you as the syntax of our self-expression,
Stringing together our words and actions
Into a lived utterance of love.

Holy Spirit, you are Advocate,
Articulate in our speechlessness, the medium of our conversation,
Interpreting, each to the other, our silences, our loss-for-words.

In you we understand each other,
Because in you, absolutely, we are understood.
O vast, attentive hinterland of our chatter,
Teach us how to listen, as well as talk,
To receive as well as transmit.

In you the words that flit between us,
Zig-zagging the short distance from soul to soul
As we tread our road together,
Can bind our mere shared direction into a single, shared journey,
And our introverted rehearsals, our dislocated speech,
Into a shared story, of where we have been
And where we are going, in you.

Readings

Genesis 18:22–33	*Abraham pleads*
Ruth 1:7–18	*Ruth convinces Naomi*
2 Kings 2:1–15	*Elijah and Elisha discuss*
Job 42:1–6	*Job repents*
Mark 12:28–34	*Question and answer*
Luke 24:13–35	*Talk on the road*
John 4:1–29	*Inter-faith dialogue*

Prayer Activity

Flick through a magazine until your eyes light on a sympathetic face – someone you feel you could talk to. Why? What does this person draw out of you that you might wish to say to a complete stranger? Light on another face, in the same magazine or another. Try this a few times. In each case, take the humanity of the person whose face it is as seriously as you can. Or – with the same respect for their humanity – do this with a face you don't immediately warm to. How much of our reaction to others do we foist on them? How ready are we for a dialogue – and how free, or otherwise, from a monologue already going on in our heads?

Prayer for the Church

As we endeavour to communicate Christianity in meaningful ways through the mass media

especially website managers, Press Officers, those involved with the production of Life & Work, E-news, Minister's Forum and in Saint Andrew Press.

Blessing

May the language of our bodies
Be the love of Christ,
The constant discourse of our gestures
His accepting welcome;
May we articulate,
In all we say, and do, and are,
The presence of Christ in his world;
And may the peace of Christ give us humility
To listen ...

MANNA – FOOD FOR THE JOURNEY

*'I am going to rain bread from heaven for you, and each day the people shall go out
and gather enough for that day. In that way I will test them, whether they will follow my
instruction or not.'*

~ Exodus 16:4 ~

These are testing times, God.

Every bit of news is bleak and ominous:
'Redundancy, recession, debt and devastation.'

Everyday the rain pours, dark and depressing:
'Cold snap, worst for years, stay in if you can.'

Every silver lining has a cloud:
'Just when you thought the end was in sight, now this.'

Like the Israelites we wonder:
Were we better off before?
What's the point of being here?
Can we take any more?

God forgive our lack of hope,
our short memory,
our selfish perspective.
For you hear our cries,
in the midst of our panic and complaints you speak:
spurring us on, opening the road
saying
enough for today, enough for today,
if you will journey – I will provide.

Readings

Matthew 4:1–11	*The temptation of Jesus*
John 6:25–59	*Jesus the Bread of Life*

Prayer Activity

Prayer for the Church

As we care for people in community who need social support and fulfil Christ's command to love our neighbour

especially those involved in the Social Care Council and its practical wing 'Crossreach', with caring units across Scotland.

Blessing

> Eat this bread, drink this cup,
> Come to me and never be hungry.
> Eat this bread, drink this cup,
> Trust in me and you will not thirst.

CH4 661 (Taize community)

HOSPITALITY

Do not neglect to show hospitality to strangers, for by doing that some have entertained angels without knowing it.

~ Hebrews 13:2 ~

Hospitality
A pause on the journey
A place of welcome
Encounter, exchange

Hospitality
A watering hole for the Spirit
A place of nourishment
Renewed, refreshed

Hospitality
A sanctuary for the fearful
A place of safe haven
Restful, secure

Hospitality
An oasis for those in the wilderness
A place of shelter to
Ponder, wonder

Lord Jesus
Host of the table
Host to the pilgrim
Journeying with us to those breathing spaces of welcome
That feed us enough to set us out again.

Following your example
May we too play host and hospitaller
Opening the doors of our hearts and homes to
Family
Friends
Strangers
And maybe, without knowing it,
the occasional Angel.

Readings

Genesis 18:1–16	*Abraham and Sarah welcoming strangers in the desert*
Deuteronomy 10:18–19	*Ancient rule of hospitality and community*
Psalm 84	*How lovely is your dwelling place*
Psalm 113	
John 13:1–20	*Mary of Bethany anoints Jesus*
Luke 10:1–12	*Sending out of the 72*
Luke 14:7–14	*Parable of the wedding feast*

Prayer Activity

Where are the places that you would call home? What makes a place feel safe and secure? Who or what makes a place a hospitable place to be and or stay? Think through the hospitable people and places of your life journey and give thanks for them.

Prayer for the Church

The Community which surrounds our Church building and from which our congregation is drawn – its commercial, agricultural and recreational institutions and residential areas

especially the support and advice provided through the Parish Development Fund and Emerging Ministries Fund to encourage good church/community interaction.

Blessing

We saw a stranger yesterday.
We put food in the eating place,
drink in the drinking place,
music in the listening place
and in the sacred name of the triune God
He blessed us and our house,
our cattle and our dear ones.
As the lark says in her song:
Often, often, often goes Christ in the stranger's guise.

~ Celtic rune of hospitality ~

BAGGAGE

The Lord is my shepherd, I shall not want. He makes me lie down in green pastures; he leads me beside still waters; he restores my soul. He leads me in right paths for his name's sake.

~ Psalm 23:1–3 ~

I shall not want.
Yet we cling fast
to what is ours, Lord.
We are too good
at zipping up the past,
padlocking the present,
and storing it within tomorrow's hopes.

I shall not want.
Yet here we are
with our excess baggage, Lord,
weighty from fears and failings,
grudges and gripes,
insecurities and uncertainties,
and little space to squeeze you in.

More than once, Lord,
you sit on grassy banks
and give, in simple stories and blessings,
the only food we need.
More than once,
you still stormy seas with mere words,
and steer your people
to a leaner, better place.
More than once,
you call us on a journey
and equip us for the road ahead
with nothing but promises.
More than once,
your uncomplicated touch calms the chaos
at the core of restless souls.

May we not want,
may we not need,
may we not ask, Lord,

for any more
than to be led by you.
And may, in your leading,
be our leaving behind.

Readings

Genesis 12:1–3	*Call of Abram*
Joshua 3:14–17	*Crossing the Jordan*
Matthew 6:25–34	*Do not worry about tomorrow*
Luke 9:1–6	*Jesus sends out the twelve*

Prayer Activity

Jesus recognised and taught the richness, the abundance of simplicity. Reflect on and give thanks for the simple things in your life that you consider real treasures. Pray also for those aspects of your life you feel may hold you back from a simpler relationship with God.

Prayer for the Church

Centres of theological study and research, their teaching-staff and students, and those considering a future life of full-time Christian service

especially the Ministries Council as they assist ministry call, discernment, formation, care and support of parish staff including parish ministers.

Blessing

When we want, Lord,
Remind us of your poverty.
When we need, Lord,
Remind us of your selflessness.
When we would have it all, Lord,
Remind us that in you we do.
Bless us and bring us, Lord,
Just as we are,
Into your presence and safekeeping,
Today and always.   AMEN.

COMPANIONS ON THE ROAD

Two are better than one because they have a good reward for their toil.

~ Ecclesiastes 4:9 ~

Journeying the many twists and turns of a life and faith journey
Longing for straight pathways where the way ahead is visible and clear

> Anam Cara, Soul Friend
> Accompany me
> Be my bread to nourish the body
> My companion to nourish the soul

Journeying in one direction while everyone else seems to move in another
 The cost of a prophetic voice is often a lonely pathway

> Anam Cara, Soul Friend
> Accompany me
> Be my bread to nourish the body
> My companion to nourish the soul

Journeying through the mist and fog, where dark shadows engulf
The sheer heavy weight and effort to lift one foot in front of another seems unbearable

> Anam Cara, Soul Friend
> Accompany me
> Be my bread to nourish the body
> My companion to nourish the soul

Journeying the sometimes inner turmoil or celebrating the joyous highs
You mirror and affirm within, the inner wisdom that knows God

> Anam Cara, Soul Friend
> Accompany me
> Be my bread to nourish the body
> My companion to nourish the soul

Readings

1 Samuel 18:1–9	*Jonathan and David*
Acts 13, 14	*Paul and Barnabas*
Luke 24:13–6	*The walk to Emmaus*
Ruth	*Ruth and Naomi*
Genesis 12, 15	*Abraham and Sarah*
2 Kings 2	*Elijah and Elisha*

Prayer Activity

So whom do you turn to when you want to reflect on aspects of your life and faith? Do you regularly spend time with a Spiritual Director or Soul Friend who will help you reflect on your prayer life and how/where God is moving in your life? Or is there a friend/companion that you turn to for a chat when needed? Reflect on the people who have accompanied you on the different stages of your faith journey – what was it about them that has helped you deepen your faith and your understanding of God?

Prayer for the Church

As we meet in local Church councils where support is given and policies made

especially your Presbytery, its clerk, moderator and work of committees. Your own elders as they meet regularly in Kirk Session and serve your congregation.

Blessing

Bread to nourish,
Friend to accompany,
Conversation to inspire,
Space to listen,
Time to reflect,
Choices to make.
Bless these gifts of the journey.

Departures

'Will you go where you don't know and never be the same ...?'
(*CH4* 533)

Journeys aren't always defined by their destination. Some of our most important journeys are defined by their point of departure. Where we left, *why* we left, what we decided we had to leave behind, what we were prised away from by circumstance or the actions of others, the 'simple fact' (hardly *simple!*) that we couldn't stay – or that we just had to go (two different things!), or the simple fact (and sometimes it *is* that simple!) that it was just *time to go* ... All these circumstances and more, define some of the most important journeys we make – or realise we *have made*.

Deepest of all, we are in the end defined *as human beings* by a departing that lies ahead of us all, and with which we have somehow to come to terms. The departing of those we love frames our own mortality, like all the departures we experience. 'You can't stay here ...' Yet faith can understand what from our perspective *has* to seem like a departure, as arrival. Dietrich Bonhoeffer's last recorded words, to his fellow prisoners, before he was hanged by the Nazis in 1945, were 'This is the end – for me the beginning of life.' Jesus says: 'When I go and prepare a place for you, I will come again and will take you to myself, that where I am you may be also.' (John 14:3)

Just so can our departure become our destination.

SEND-OFFS

Then after fasting and praying they laid their hands on them and sent them off.

~ Acts 13:3 ~

Goodbye!
Some folk say 'goodbye'
about five times before they part.
Others mutter incoherently,
signing off, as they walk away.
The intimate sometimes say nothing,
presuming the inevitability of meeting again.

Goodbye –
originally: 'God be with you.'
Yes, every goodbye
is a blessing – in theory –
but to be practised
involves the heart as well as lips.
And, of course,
some 'goodbyes' are hellish
but then
maybe they
are the ones that need most blessing.

We all love a good send-off!
It makes us feel better to know
that we have done all we can
to make the leaving a celebration.
It is important to leave well.
It is important to let others leave well.
Leaving is an integral part of a relationship.
And all relationships are bounded
by the constancy of our journey
into Your life, O God.

Your Story Book is full of send-offs
that are accompanied by blessing.
So, help us to say our goodbyes
in the way that befits us as children of God.
For wherever we go,
You are there already.

Readings

Genesis 28:1–5	*Isaac blesses Jacob and sends him off to his mother's brother*
Joshua 1:1–9	*God sends off Joshua with assurance of His constant presence*
Luke 8:26–39	*The exorcised man is sent home by Jesus to witness there*
Matthew 28:16–20	*The ultimate send-off to go and evangelise the world*
Acts 1:6–11	*The ascension of Jesus*
Acts 13:1–5	*Barnabas and Saul are commissioned and sent off*

Prayer Activity

Dare to try an experiment. For one day, instead of saying 'goodbye', say 'God be with you' in its place and pray for the other person. Ask them for a blessing in response if it is appropriate.

In the evening, reflect .... what difference did it make? Should your experiment become a habit?

Prayer for the Church

Those who have gone out from our own congregation to serve the Christian Church elsewhere, in this country and overseas

especially those of the World Mission Council who offer sustained contact with missionary partners and missionary churches (see list of names at rear of book).

Blessing

May the blessings of the Lord
fill all your 'hellos' and 'goodbyes',
until the day
Your name is hallowed
at the gates of heaven.

EXODUS – MOSES

They said to Moses, 'Was it because there were no graves in Egypt that you have taken us away to die in the wilderness? What have you done to us, bringing us out of Egypt? Is this not the very thing we told you in Egypt, Let us alone and let us serve the Egyptians? For it would have been better for us to serve the Egyptians than to die in the wilderness.' But Moses said to the people, 'Do not be afraid, stand firm, and see the deliverance that the LORD will accomplish for you today; for the Egyptians whom you see today you shall never see again.

~ Exodus 14:11–13 ~

I advocated faith, Lord, called them to believe –
    And now, faith separates me from them.
I said 'Trust!' – when none of us knew
What a huge thing – a thin thing – trust is;
    When everything was going well,
The past with its problems so easy to leave behind.
Out we marched, and forward, our problems dissolved;
    And, suddenly, it has come to this!
How did we get here, to this godforsaken place,
    This narrow and narrowing strip
    Between unstoppable threat and immovable obstacle?
    That is what they are asking, Lord, of you – and of me.
I ask it of myself, of course. Was faith too glib,
    Trust too easy, triumphant language the tongue's to command?
    Did I know what I was saying? Implying? *Promising?*
None of it has turned out as we imagined
    Yet now, I *know* that *all of it* is in your hand.
    I can and do still trust your promise:
Not a way out – there is none. Nor a way round – this is too big,
    Too swamping a reality.
A way through? If we face this. If we take it upon ourselves, in trust,
    You will make this dead stop
    Into a part of our journey with you.
So let me believe, Lord – for them. For all of us …

Readings

Exodus 3:1–15	*God calls Moses*
Exodus 14:1–14	*Crossing the Red Sea*
2 Kings 6:11–23	*The defeat of an army*
Luke 9:28–36	*Who is my neighbour?*
Luke 22: 39–46	*Jesus prays*

Prayer Activity

Turn your chair to face a wall. Contemplate its solidity, there in front of you, the obstacle it presents to your going that way. Spend some time doing this. Now turn and contemplate a closed door. The door will open, if you approach it. Which situations, in your life, or in the life of the world, feel like a doorway yet to be opened? Which feel 'like a brick wall'? Make a list, mental or written, of each kind, and pray about them. Is it possible that you are wrong about which are 'doors' and which are 'brick walls'?

Prayer for the Church

Finance: Recalling individual and national situations that can affect housing, employment, family welfare as well as industry, banking and world economics

especially people who advise the Church with regard to investments and pensions or are employed in Stewardship & Finance or the General Treasurers department.

Blessing

The God of the Exodus give to us
The wisdom to know
When we must turn back,
The humility to know
When we must go round,
And the faith to know
When we have to go through,
And the trust that he will come with us,
If we will go with him.

CASTING NETS ON THE OTHER SIDE

This was now the third time that Jesus appeared to the disciples after he was raised from the dead.

~ John 21:14 ~

Deep in thought, burdened by despair ...
Did those disciples stare into the water and see themselves?

No fish, no prospects,
Nothing working,
No way.
Just themselves.

Did they feel helpless?

No idea, no skill,
Nothing working,
No way.
Just themselves.

God, I wonder if they felt like I do sometimes?
Faced with myself
Weak and alone
No way.

Yet, in that reflection I see your creation –
The creation of hope and possibility.
And Jesus comes to invite and excite,
To offer help and alternatives –
Pushing the boundaries,
calling for the other side to be explored,
showing a new way.

God thank you that with Christ there are no dead ends.
Thank you for showing us that way:
Abundantly giving,
Amazingly loving,
Astoundingly showing
Love, that never leaves us
And leads
To life in all its fullness.   AMEN.

Readings

Genesis 2:26–31   *Human beings created*
Luke 19:1–9   *A change seen in Zacchaeus*
Psalm 139   *God's perspective*

Prayer Activity

Stand in front of a mirror and hold another mirror behind your head and to the side. As you look at these different ways of seeing yourself, think about how others see you and how God does – let that different perspective make a difference to your day.

Prayer for the Church

For young adults faced with choices of lifestyle, peer pressures while setting life priorities including spiritual direction, and those who offer them guidance

especially CoSY, the Youth Assembly, 25+ church and those who organise these, along with Christian youth workers across the country.

Blessing

Take, oh, take me as I am;
Summon out what I shall be;
set your seal upon my heart
and live in me.

CH4 794

ASYLUM

'Then the fugitive shall be taken into the city, and given a place, and shall remain with them.'

~ Joshua 20:4b ~

Thy will be done.
Fugitives from injustice
deserve sanctuary,
inviolable refuge
from persecution or oppression.
Each asylum seeker given
welcome and fair hearing.

And as those bloodied feet in ancient times
fled along safety-seeking roads,
so the flights continue
in the desperation-driven refugee
suffering the suffocating darkness of the ship's hold
or bearing the battering in the hidden depths of the lorry's load.

And then arrival!
Bent figures –
hungry, thirsty, bewildered, frightened
and with
nothing
but a hope, a dream
that things might be better here!

No room at the inn of the city –
Christ, those words after such journeying –
but we have a place round the back.
You may call it a stable
but we call it a detention centre.

Surely new life can begin anywhere?
Isn't that what the Gospel's about?

O God, help us to make our city
one of Your cities of refuge and justice.
It's the least we can do in Jesus' name.
His cruciform arms embrace
every asylum seeker
and there is room for everyone.

Readings

Prayer Activity

Think! What are your ten most precious possessions? Imagine having to leave your home and country and you cannot take any of them with you. When you arrived in the new place, what would you most need? Now give thanks for what you have and pray for those who arrive here with nothing.

Prayer for the Church

Those who remind us that 'the world belongs unto the Lord' and that we are stewards and carers for creation

especially those involved with the eco-congregations' project, church energy conservation and local 'recyclers'.

Blessing

> Bless
> finders and keepers,
> losers and weepers,
> hiders and seekers
> that all may be found
> in the Kingdom of God;
> a place of asylum
> called Love of the Lord.

BEREAVEMENT

But the man of God said, 'Let her alone, for she is in bitter distress; the LORD has hidden it from me and has not told me.'

~ 2 Kings 4:27 ~

Blessed are those who mourn, for they will be comforted.

~ Matthew 5:4 ~

Everything has stopped. I am going nowhere.
I used to have to guess what grief was. I'm still not sure.
All I know now is this:
Grief is the impress, the stamp, the crushing impact
Of a huge-beyond-words reality of loss
On the fragile thing which is, it turns out, me.

I didn't think I was so small, so fragile.
Suddenly, I don't know myself;
So much of what I thought I knew
Has also died. I didn't think it would be like this, *could* be like this…
But I don't feel as though I have moved an inch from where I was.

Very precisely, it's *not about me*.
It is *the loss* that is all-consuming,
The *one I've lost* who is everything.

The truth is, I'm not ready for consolation yet;
Not ready to be moved on by someone else's nervous, pitying agenda.
(I'm sorry. They mean well.)
Not ready – God forbid! – for *closure*. The wounds are still open.
But – stay with me, Lord.
I seem to sense – and need to know –
That somehow it was like this for you, too;
That *God knew grief.*
That sounds like the sort of thing
Learned divines would laugh at, or cry *'Heresy!'*
All I know is this:
'Only the suffering God can help …'*

Can you help me, Lord? Do you really know what it's like to be here?

'Jesus wept …' I can cling to that. I can stay here a while,
And perhaps, at length, from here move on.

* Dietrich Bonhoeffer, *Letters and Papers from Prison*, SCM Press, 1967, p. 197.

Readings

Prayer Activity

Someone once said that being bereaved is like living in a beach-house. Every morning, you go down to the beach – and you have no idea how it is going to be. Some mornings, the sand is strewn with the flotsam and seaweed of last night's storm; some mornings, the fog has rolled in, and you can see practically nothing; some mornings are beautiful, pristine, magical and deeply consoling; some mornings the tide is right in, and the beach is a confined, frustrated, uncomfortable strip of sand. Does this – in particular the *randomness* of the succession of days – resonate with your experience? Does it *help?* In particular – does it set you free from other people's expectations (and maybe your own) of how you *should* feel about loss? Bring all this to God.

Prayer for the Church

For those who create worship materials, those who deliver them to us and for ourselves as active and expectant participants

especially for the Worship and Doctrine Taskgroup, the CH4 trustees, The Wild Goose Worship group of the Iona Community, Worship-on-the web contributors and for worship leaders in our congregation.

Blessing

> May God, who is with you where you are,
> Who waits with you in the silence
> To which none of our anxious words are equal,
> bless you:
> And when he shall speak the word
> That none but God can speak
> You shall be consoled.

Emotional Journeys

Emotional journeys can leave us feeling as if we have just run a marathon. We may be elated, relieved, distraught or simply drained and exhausted. Unlike external journeys, there are no maps for the internal ones. But as with all personalised travel, we make our own detours and stops along the way. Sometimes we get where we want to be. Sometimes we break down. Often we long for an emotional 'sat-nav' that tell us how to feel at any given moment and how to make sense of things.

The stories of Jesus show us an emotional, real-life human being who weeps, becomes angry and struggles with temptations. And in all his emotional turmoil, He is sustained by God the Father.

Jesus sent the Holy Spirit to be our internal companion. She is always with us. And emotions are a gift –

I feel
therefore
I am alive!

LAMENT

'I am weary with my moaning;
every night I flood my bed with tears;
I drench my couch with my weeping.'

~ Psalm 6:6 ~

God,
Sometimes
all there is…
is tears.

An aching,
an emptiness,
an experience of abandonment.
The loss of someone we loved,
the end of something that gave
life meaning,
the absence of You.

Sometimes
the only response
is tears.

In the face
of my helplessness,
nothing
I can do or say
to help
or to mend
another's broken-ness.

So tears
may be
the only meaningful,
meaning-laden
response.

Jesus wept.

So why might I
resist
or regret
such a natural
expression of sorrow
or act of compassion?

Readings

Job 2:11–13	*Job's comforters' initial response to his suffering*
John 11:28–37	*Jesus' response to the grief of Mary and her friends*
Luke 19:41f	*Jesus weeps over Jerusalem*
Matthew 27:45–50	*'My God, my God, why have you forsaken me?'*

Prayer Activity

In church circles and wider society we can get the feeling that to shed tears is to be weak or is a sign of not coping. Our readings from the Old Testament and from the Gospels contradict this. Tears can be a relief, a release of a build up of tension or a natural human response to loss and suffering which reveals how we really feel for, and about, another in situations when words are inadequate. In the quiet, remember times when tears have been a release for you or when the tears of others have been a comfort or brought solace. Thank God for the gift of tears.

Prayer for the Church

Those concerned with government at international, national, regional and local levels

especially the Church and Society Council, the Scottish Churches Parliamentary Office and my elected representatives in government.

Blessing

May the love of the Wounded Healer,
The compassion of the Christ who wept,
The gentleness of our Companion along the Way,
Surround you and those whom you love,
This day, this night and forevermore.   AMEN.

LONGING

As a deer longs for flowing streams, so my soul longs for you, O God.

~ Psalm 42:1 ~

God,
What is life about?
I mean I do my best
I work hard ... well most of the time...
at relationships,
at trying to contribute –
in work, at home, at church and in the community.
I care for family and friends.
Sure, I slip up sometimes, everyone does,
but I pick myself up and try to do better next time.

God,
What is life about?
Sometimes there seems no purpose to it at all,
a never-ending treadmill –
and I'm the hamster.
It's the same routine, and often that's just fine,
but sometimes ...
sometimes it's just not enough.
Is there more?

God,
I don't know what's missing.
I'm not sure what I need,
what I really desire.

So show me, God,
come close and ease that
empty ache which gnaws away inside me ...
That longing for
fullness and fulfilment in life,
that deep need to belong and be loved ...
as I am.   AMEN.

Readings

Songs of Solomon 7:10	*'I am my beloved's, and his desire is for me.'*
Matthew 3:17	*'And a voice from heaven said "This is my beloved Son with whom I am well pleased."'*
Isaiah 62:5	*'... as the bridegroom rejoices over the bride, so shall your God rejoice over you.'*

Prayer Activity

Sit or lie quietly and let your mind take you to the banks of the Jordan. Feel the heat of the sun, the grains of the sand between your toes, the warmth of the lapping water around your feet. It is you who is being baptised by John, it is you on whom the Spirit of God descends and it is you to whom the voice of heaven says 'You ... (say your name) ... you are my beloved son/daughter and I am well pleased with you.' Repeat this quietly to yourself several times. Let this realisation wash over you ....you are loved, you do belong to God ... just as you are.

Prayer for the Church

All those currently serving in our armed forces, at home or overseas, and those veterans and their families who have experienced tragedy through trauma, death and injury

especially Chaplains with Army, Royal Navy, Royal Air Force, Territorial and cadet units.

Blessing

In our lives and our longing, God,
In our seeking and our searching, Christ,
In the depths of our desire, Holy Spirit;

God Three-in-one,
Loving us,
Offering fulfilment for us
Leading us on...

DEAD-ENDS

But Jonah set out to flee to Tarshish from the presence of the Lord.

~ Jonah 1:3a ~

I find it difficult to accept dead-ends.
I have grown to believe that with faith
I can get through any situation,
that every path will lead me somewhere.
And so when I come up against a wall
and can move no further
I waste time searching for an opening.
Then I try to climb over
and when all else fails
I stand and hammer it with childish fists
in case it will come tumbling down
like the walls of Jericho!

I cannot bear to hit the wall
in my relationships or in my work.
I feel a failure.
Teach me Lord,
when I find myself in a cul-de-sac
to reflect on how I got there.

Occasionally relationships are best severed
for the creative good of both parties.
So hard!
Sometimes you call us away from one kind of work to another.
Some things are meant to be stopped!
Any path forged out of vengeance, deceit or betrayal,
or littered with greed and sinful self-indulgence
is bound to lead to a dead-end.

And having reflected as Jonah did,
I will turn to You, God,
and pray that You will deliver me
from the belly of the whale
to once again journey towards life.

Readings

Jonah 1, 2, 3:1–3	*Jonah flees from God to the dead-end of a whale's belly*
Luke 15:11–20	*The prodigal son journeys to the hell of his own making*
Matthew 26:14–16, 47–50	
& 27:3–5	*Judas cannot undo what he has done.*
Acts 5:1–10	*Ananias and Sapphira discover the deadliness of deceit*

Prayer Activity

Have you ever found yourself in a 'cul-de-sac'? Did it feel like a dead-end, or more like a holding place, or a turning place, or a growing place? Pray for those who believe themselves to have reached a dead-end. Remember that wherever you are, God is. God's intention is that none should be left at a dead-end.

Prayer for the Church

Those who guide the Church in matters of law and justice and ensure all that we do is in accordance with the law and best practice

especially the Church's Law department, Safeguarding Unit and Health & Safety office.

Blessing

God bless our advancing,
God bless our retreating
God bless our traversing
God bless our homecoming.

SOLITUDE

And after he dismissed the crowds he went the mountain by himself to pray.

~ Matthew 14:23 ~

God,
sometimes like your Son,
I need to be alone;
to let things sink in,
to get my head around what has happened,
to work things out,
to let things…
and me
be.

God,
Sometimes like your Son,
I endure desert places,
on my own,
alone in a bewildering landscape with no cairns or signposts
to orientate or point the way.

God,
Sometimes like your Son,
I find moments…
in amongst the crowd,
in amongst the daily tasks
in amongst the chatter and noise…
life-enhancing moments
when we connect
You and me.

God,
Sometimes like your Son,
I feel alone and afraid,
even in the company of friends.
Friends who mean well,
who care but don't understand
or don't have the energy,
courage or insight
to wait with me.

God,
Sometimes like your Son,
I manage to get the balance
when being in solitude with You
is part of my daily and weekly rhythm.

God,
These are times in my life, real times.
May I know these are times in your Son's life too.   AMEN.

Readings

John 4:1–11   *Temptation of Jesus*
Luke 9:18   *Jesus praying by himself in the company of his disciples*
Matthew 26:36–45   *Jesus seeks company in his solitude*

Prayer (or Pre-prayer) Activity

What we need, wrote Thomas Merton in *Conjectures of a Guilty Bystander*, 'is to trifle and vegetate without feeling guilty about it.' In our weekly rhythm we need periods of passivity as well as activity. Going from work, church activities, caring for others and household chores to the other extreme of stillness, silence and prayer is far from easy. Making time to 'chill out' or 'veg' is not just about relaxing and unwinding; it is also preparation for prayer. Make time today to do nothing but watch the television, read, listen to music or watch the view from a window. Now pray.

Prayer for the Church

Remembering those who often feel they live on the fringe of society and are fearful for their well-being, sometimes because we exclude them, wittingly or otherwise, from our fellowship

especially the work of the HIV/AIDS project group and those who live with this condition in their own bodies, or amongst those whom they love.

Blessing

In our relating and our doing,
In our unwinding and relaxing
In our solitude and struggling
God's blessing.

AWARENESS

'There (Mount Horeb) the angel of the Lord appeared to him in a flame of fire out of a bush; he looked and the bush was blazing, yet it was not consumed. Then Moses said, 'I must turn aside and look at this great sight, and see why the bush is not burned up.'

~ Exodus 3:2–3 ~

O God,
turning aside,
stopping and stooping ...
to look and listen,
I might glimpse You.

Curiosity,
an intentional gaze,
an attentive ear;
gives opportunity
for transcendence.

Yet so often
I rush by
without a second glance,
iPod or plans for the day
wired into my consciousness.

Holy ground missed,
Gut feelings ignored,
Voices, within and without,
Blanked.
Too busy, tired, or preoccupied.

O God,
in being aware
of numinous possibilities
in ordinary moments...
I can encounter you.

Readings

Luke 19:5	*Jesus' encounter with Zaccheus*
Luke 8:46	*Jesus' encounter with the woman with heavy bleeding*
Habakkuk 2:3	*Waiting attentively*
Mark 10:46f	*Blind Bartimaeus*

Prayer Activity

The priest-poet R. S. Thomas described the essence of life not as hurrying through the present moment to reach a hoped for goal or future but as 'turning aside like Moses to see the miracle of the lit bush.' As I write this I am looking out at a bright red azalea bush in the garden and Moses' example encourages me to set aside my typing and to go outside and enjoy its beauty. What have you seen today but not really observed, listened to but not really heard and felt but not taken notice of? Ask God to help you be attentive, to turn aside in your time of quiet and see, hear and discern the miracle of the moment.

Prayer for the Church

Those involved in a healing ministry, Christian Counselling and Hospital and Hospice Chaplaincy

especially the Christian Fellowship of Healing and local prayer groups within your own parish.

Blessing

God be in my ears, and in my hearing;
God be in my eyes, and in my seeing;
God be in my gut and my discerning;
God be in my heart, and in my feeling;
God be in my head and in my understanding.

Transitions

Our lives are often in transition – moving from one place to another. Transition implies change and movement, something that may bring challenge, excitement and renewed energy; but, equally, transition can be that frustrating time of waiting, a time that unsettles us in the not knowing.

In times of transition we often reach out to God, seeking some sense of guidance, meaning and purpose in our lives. Is this the right job for me? Where should I be living and working? Does this relationship bring out the best in me? Our questioning allows transition to become a fruitful experience when we can listen attentively to the prompting of the Holy Spirit. A time to be still, to take stock, of our lives and maybe, to move on in a new or different direction.

Transition is often a time of letting go, leaving behind some things or some people, a time to rest in the presence of God, a time to discern the next stage of the journey, until we are ready to embrace the new and to welcome it home.

WAITING ON

Now after they (the wise men) had left, an angel of the Lord appeared to Joseph in a dream and said, 'Get up, take the child and his mother, and flee to Egypt, and remain there until I tell you: for Herod is about to search for the child, to destroy him.'

~ Matthew 2:13 ~

God,
At times my journey –
through a day or a relationship,
through a holiday or my career,
through my retirement
               … my lifetime –
doesn't go according to plan.
I've the route worked out,
the resources I require,
a timescale in mind
a destination to reach,
or a goal to achieve …
but
the road ahead becomes blurred
or blocked
due to events beyond my ken or control.

Change or illness slow me down,
an accident or ending
stops me in my tracks.
Threat of danger or loss
force me to think again.

A time of listening …
                a time of discerning,
a difficult yet necessary time
… the waiting time.

Until life unravels,
events unfold,
and emotions calm.

Clarity creeps up on me,
is glimpsed or grasped.

Voices from within and without
are weighed up ...
a decision gestates.

Perhaps, once underway again,
travelling to the same,
different or even unknown
destination,
the journeying may be more
mindful,
meaningful
and at a more appropriate pace.

Readings

Matthew 2:13f	*Joseph and Mary wait in Egypt until circumstances change*
Psalm 130:5–8	*Waiting on and hoping in God*
Isaiah 40:27f	*Those who wait for the Lord shall renew their strength*
Lamentations 3:25–6	*The Lord is good to those who wait for him*

Prayer Activity

In your prayers and in the quiet let the situation or choices you have ... be ... and wait. Ask God for wisdom, guidance and discernment. Mull over the advice of trusted others, the various ideas and possibilities that spring to mind and the feelings that arise when you imagine yourself going down a possible path.

Prayer for the Church

Christian organisations that promote life-long Christian learning, fellowship and service

especially the Church of Scotland Guild, at national and local levels.

Blessing

In my waiting, God, grant me patience
In my discerning, God, help me listen
In my choosing, God, give me wisdom
In the way forward, God, be my companion.

CONVERSION

Saul got up from the ground, and though his eyes were open, he could see nothing; so they led him by the hand and brought him into Damascus.

~ Acts 9:8 ~

The light that blinded me has made me see,
That before, I could *not* see,
Nor had I been looking...

The road I travelled so confidently
Promising to take me where my real business was –
Its every mile informed by *my* purpose, *my* itinerary –
Is suddenly a detour I now stumble along...

The destination I was so sure of reaching,
Because I knew what I wanted to do when I got there,
Is now no goal, but just 'what's next' in my wandering ...

And yet:
In my blindness I am glimpsing truth – at last.
In my lostness – at last – I know at least where I am *not*.
My very aimlessness – *my* goal, *my* purpose now snatched away –
Are inklings of *your* purpose for me.

And still I journey on, to where I was going,
Because now, when I get there, I *will know*
That this was never where I was really going,
Never to be the end of my journeying...

A conversion, a turning-around – yet still I travel in the same direction.
What has changed? Nothing – and everything.

You stood in my way, and would not let me pass;
Not as the 'me' I was.
So I give up what I was, yield myself to you.
Walk with me now, and teach me who I am; help me to accept what I shall be.
For who I am, and who I shall be, are yours to give.

Readings

Numbers 22:1 – 23:12   *The King sends for Balaam*
2 Kings 5:15–19   *Naaman is cured*
Matthew 9:9–13   *Jesus calls Matthew*
Luke 19:1–10   *Jesus and Zacchaeus*
Acts 9:1–9   *The Conversion of Saul*
2 Corinthians 12:1–11   *Paul's Visions and Revelations*
Philippians 3:2–17   *The True Righteousness*

Prayer Activity

A simple but effective monkey trap is made like this; take a jar with a narrow neck, place a nut in it, and tie it to a stake. The key is that the neck of the jar must be wide enough for a monkey's open hand, but not his clenched fist. Eventually a monkey will come along and investigate, and, detecting the nut, will reach in his arm to grab it. But he won't be able to bring himself to let go of his prize, and so he will be caught.

Clench your fist. What are you holding? What is holding you fast? What can't you relinquish, to accept the freedom that God offers in Christ? Prayerfully seek to identify it – then let go of it.

Prayer for the Church

Imaginative and spiritually astute vision that enables the Christian Church to engage with 21st-century challenges and opportunities

especially those concerned with Panel on Review and Reform, 'Future Focus' facilitators, Church Without Walls and Council of Assembly.

Blessing

*'Let me no more my comfort draw
From my frail grasp of thee;
In this alone rejoice with awe
Thy mighty grasp of me.'*

John Campbell Shairp

God tease from our grasp
The things that hold us fast
So that we may know his grasp of us
In the freedom of faith, that binds us to him.

BEYOND THE BOUNDARIES

Now the Lord said to Abram, 'Go from your country and your kindred and your father's house to the land that I will show you.

~ Genesis 12:1 ~

Sometimes, our journeys take us
Beyond the boundaries of our comfort zone
Into that unfamiliar place or experience
And we find ourselves
At that turning point
Where choices are made.

Stepping out
Moving on
Saying farewells
Acknowledging fear
Containing excitement
Embracing the unknown

Sometimes, things are clearer to see
outside the box of our comfort zone
stepping out from a familiar place or experience
and we find ourselves
with a prophetic voice or vision
chipping away at the edges.

So as we journey into ventures new
Trusting in your guiding Spirit
Seeking your presence,
Like Abram, we find that
God, you are with us in the familiar place
God, you are with us in the unknown place
In this place and that place
In every place.

Readings

Genesis 12:1- 10   *Abram and Sarai set out into the desert*
John 4:1–42   *Woman at the well*
John 21:15–20   *Jesus and Peter – feed my lambs*

Prayer Activity

Think of the turning points in your life and faith journey. What experiences led up to that sense of moving on, turning around? Try to recall the emotions, places and people involved. Where did you find God in these turning points?

Prayer for the Church

That we may worship, work and witness alongside those of a variety of denominations, recognising that the Holy Spirit of God binds us together

especially for the work of the Committee on Ecumenical relations, charities such as Christian Aid and sister congregations in our community.

Blessing

Sent by the Lord am I;
My hands are ready now
To make the earth a place
In which the kingdom comes.
The angels cannot change
A world of hurt and pain
Into a world of love,
Of justice and of peace.
The task is mine to do,
to set it really free.

MARY, MOTHER OF JESUS

And Mary said, 'My soul magnifies the Lord, and my spirit rejoices in God my Saviour, for he has looked with favour on the lowliness of his servant. Surely, from now on, all generations will call me blessed; for the Mighty One has done great things for me and holy is his name.'

~ Luke 1:46–9 ~

It was that first word,
whispered in dim dream
yet as clear as a star defiant against dark,
that beckoned me on this journey, Lord.
And like Mary, I was no longer a child.

It was the strange comfort
of that stirring deep inside,
unfamiliar yet easy as an old friend,
that set me on the road, Lord.
And, like Mary, I was partner and protector.

It was the pain of deliverance,
as hopes and fears burst free,
that left space for love's ache to linger
and lead the way, Lord.
And, like Mary, I learned the value of loss.

It was the touch of the divine,
fresh and free from dirt and despair,
that soothed faith's ragged edges
as it surrendered to you, Lord.
And, like Mary, my part was plain.

Still my soul resists, my spirit struggles,
and my journey is one of joy and jarring.
As I voyage with you before, within, beside, beyond,
may I come to sing Mary's song, Lord,
and know the holiness of my humanity.

Readings

Isaiah 7:14 — *Isaiah prophesies Jesus' birth*
Matthew 12:46–50 — *Who is my mother?*
Luke 1:38 — *Mary's obedience*
John 19: 26–7 — *'Woman, here is your son'*

Prayer Activity

Think of someone who has been like a mother to you and why. Give thanks for that person and for the ways in which they have mothered you.

Prayer for the Church

Remembering the variety of setting of the Christian Church in our land – rural and remote – city centre – priority area – town or village and their differing needs

especially the Priorities Areas ministry team, the Scottish Churches Rural Strategy group, work in Parish grouping and of Presbytery planning teams.

Blessing

Love has made us
Love has shaped us
Love has shown us the way.
May we go from here
Knowing we are held for eternity
By a love like no other
To share love with one another
In Jesus' name.   AMEN.

CALLING

...and he said to him, 'follow me'. And he got up, left everything, and followed him.

~ Luke 5:27–8 ~

From the shores of Lake Galilee,
The tables of Tax Collectors,
Encounters on the roadside,
You invited the unlikeliest of men to be your disciples with a summons
'Come and follow me'

In the silence of the night time
As visions interrupt sleep and dreams
When angels gathered to sing their praises
You called the unlikeliest of women and children to respond
'Yes Lord! I am listening'

With the great cloud of witnesses gone before us
We too settle into the stillness of the quiet, to listen for your call

And so we wait,
Attentive to the prompting of the Spirit:
A closed door begins to creak open
The nudging of a friend encourages new possibility
A repeating word irritates and resonates
A nagging disquiet interrupts daily routine
And we begin to discern where our energy and desire lies.

Here I am Lord
Waiting for your invitation
'Come and follow me.'
Not a predestined journey
But the start of an adventure
With you, the Divine Imagination.

Readings

Luke 5:1–11   *Call of the Fishermen*

Luke 5:27–32   *Call of Mathew*

Luke 1:26–38   *Mary and Gabriel*

1 Samuel 3   *Call of Samuel*

John 1:43–51   *Call of Philip and Nathaniel*

Acts 9:1–22   *Conversion of Saul*

Prayer Activity

How did you come to know God? Have you been nurtured in the faith throughout your life or was there a sudden conversion experience? How have you followed God's call? What direction has that taken you? How do you discern where God is calling you now to do and to be? Think about the places, people and situations that have shaped your calling.

Prayer for the Church

For employers, unions and those involved in matching skills and abilities with opportunities. For those under-employed and often losing self-esteem as a result

especially the Central Services Committee of the Church of Scotland, and those who occupy managerial roles.

Blessing

Lord, your summons echoes true
When you but call my name
Let me turn and follow you
And never be the same.
In your company I'll go
Where your love and footsteps show.
Thus I'll move and live and grow
In you and you in me.

CH4 533

New Directions

It isn't always where we intend to go that we wind up. Levi the tax-collector had the meaning of his whole life on the table before him, in the piles of money for which he had traded respect, friendship, even simple, everyday, human solidarity. Jesus came by. Levi got up and left it all, and became someone different. He didn't know where he was going – just that he had to go. He had reached not maybe a fork in the road, but certainly a junction. A junction offers us a choice; will we go on the way we have been, complete the journey we started – or take a new way, begin a new journey, abandon the old one? There is always the default option – carry on as before.

So we evaluate. We weigh, and measure, we ask what is important and precious to us about the road we are treading, and have been for a while now, the journey we believe we are on – and what might be better in a change of direction, a change of goal. For faith, at the point the possibility of a new direction opens up, this weighing and measuring is a deeply prayerful process. We hand all these things to God. Yet for faith, too, the choice is ours to make. He hands the decision back. We decide. Yet God is in all this.

'Your word is a lamp to my feet, and a light to my path.'

(Psalm 119:105)

SACRAMENTAL

While they were eating, he took a loaf of bread, and after blessing it he broke it, gave it to them, and said, 'Take; this is my body.' Then he took a cup, and after giving thanks he gave it to them, and all of them drank from it. He said to them, 'This is my blood of the covenant, which is poured out for many.'

~ Mark 14:22–5 ~

There are moments when
Heaven breaks into the world,
And we glimpse you, God,
Through water, bread and wine.

Water, Baptism
A time of welcome
Acting out Your love for every human being,
Washing clean all that has been.
We start life over again
Chosen by You to be one of your disciples.

Bread, wine
Holy Communion
A time for nourishment
Gathering around a table
And in that breaking bread moment
We say this is how we would like the world to be
Where everyone is fed and shares together.

These are the signs of
Your renewal God,
Your ever present Grace
That speak to us of

Of longing for justice
Sustaining us and feeding us,

Of being in the right relationship
healing us and bringing us to wholeness,

Of creation and re creating
Restoring the image of you, God, in us.

These are the moments when
Heaven breaks into the world,
And we glimpse you, God,
Reminding us that
This is how we should be,
Not just for this one moment
But for every moment
In every time, in every place.

Readings

Matthew 3 *Baptism of Jesus*
Luke 22:7–20 *The Passover meal*
Acts 19:1–7 *Baptism at Ephesus*

Prayer Activity

What are the times when you glimpse a deep sense of God's touching presence – sometimes described as 'awesome moments'? Think of the people you have met, the places you have been, situations you have found yourself in –remember them and give thanks for those moments when we glimpse heaven breaking through to earth.

Prayer for the Church

Those concerned with education and spiritual development – University and College Christian Fellowships. Chaplains in schools, colleges and universities and R.M.E teachers

especially for Adult Christian Educators, Presbytery Youth and Children trainers, elder training programmes.

Blessing

The Lord bless you and keep you;
The Lord make his face to shine upon you, and be gracious to you;
The Lord lift up his countenance upon you,
And give you peace.

Numbers 6:24

CHOICES – GETHSEMANE

Then Jesus went with them to a place called Gethsemane; and he said to his disciples, 'Sit here while I go over there and pray'. And going a little further, he threw himself on the ground and prayed, 'My Father, if it is possible, let this cup pass from me; yet not what I want but what you want.'

~ Matthew 26:36, 39 ~

Indecision is a blessing undisguised.
It forgives us our uncertainty
and graces us with time.
And so we linger at life's junctions
and seek pardon for our pondering.

No such luxury for you, Lord,
you for who confronting crossroads,
even in deserted places
and among uncomplicated souls,
was not chance but choice.

Until you reached a garden
and the fork in the road,
fogged by fear, fury and frustration,
became less clear.
Until you reached a garden
where options seemed as limited
as the wakefulness of friends.
Until you reached a garden
where you agonised
again and again,
at one final outrage.
Until you reached a garden
and made the finite choice.

Thank you for picking us, Lord,
when you had other options.
Thank you, that you took the cup
and saw your own reflection
mirrored in its ruby richness.
Thank you that you caressed
the coldness of its grip
with lips which parted in love.

Thank you that you drank its bitterness
and felt it course like blood
through living veins.

Thank you that in your indecision
we may see our struggling selves
in your divine disguise
and, in our humanity, choose you.

Readings

Joshua 24:15	*The Israelites asked to choose which god they will serve*
Matthew 16:24	*Taking up your cross*
Mark 14:10	*Judas decides to betray Jesus*
1 Peter 1:13	*Choices about how we live*

Prayer Activity

How do we see ourselves reflected in Christ? Think of the choices he made and of ways in which your actions might mirror his in the situations you encounter every day, for example, when someone asks for help, lets you down, criticises or challenges you. Pray for openness and guidance in your choices.

Prayer for the Church

Worshipping communities who live 'as strangers in a foreign land' while endeavouring to build and maintain bridges between people

especially our congregations across Europe, in Israel, and on Caribbean islands, continuing to serve English-speaking communities.

Blessing

God's love has chosen us,
God's justice has saved us,
God's grace has blessed us.
May the God of love, justice and grace
Be with us in our choices
And in our chances
This day and always.   AMEN.

ROUTINES

On the Sabbath day, we went outside the gate by the river,
where we supposed there was a place of prayer;
and we sat down and spoke to the women who had gathered there.

~ Acts 16:13 ~

Forgive me Lord.
Forgive me for the days I want to break out.
Break out from the small routine journeys I make:
to the school gates, to the bus stop, to my work,
to the shops, to church.
You see, the bottom line, is
I need these routines –
they are the mechanics of my stability.

They are warm, familiar, purpose-driven actions.
And I have chosen to do them.
Every routine little step is a journey of love into community:
Parents bonded by the challenges of bringing up a child.
Fellow commuters bonded by the frustrations of public transport.
Colleagues bonded by shared goals and playtime stories.
Shoppers bonded in their bargain-hunting and the joy of queuing!
Worshippers bonded by the Spirit and their search for grace.

One day, I will miss these routines:
For I am in the doing of them.
One day, I am sure, I will rely on others
to do unto me my routines.
Simple pleasures such as the journey
from bed to toilet to dressing to walking to eating –
will no longer be my choice alone.

When this times comes,
please Lord,
may I be gracious and humble
as I receive the little steps of love from my enablers.
May I find joy in a different kind of community.
In the meantime, thank You,
for all the 'families' to which I belong
and for the glimpses of the extraordinary in the mundane.

Readings

Mark 1:16–20	*No more routine journey to work for the four fishermen!*
John 5:1–9	*Routinely, for 38 years, a disabled man has tried to get to the healing waters*
Luke 10:38–42	*Martha's domestic routine distracts her from what is needed*
Acts 2:43–7	*The daily routine of the believers is attractive to others*

Prayer Activity

What are the routines that make up your life? What would life be like without them? Pray for those you encounter routinely. Remember those whose routines involve constant caring for a loved one, especially children, those who routinely face danger and those whose lives depend on the health routines they perform every day.

Finally, ponder on the question:
~ if we are Spirit led, can our lives ever become routine?

Prayer for the Church

For those entrusted with the care of places of worship, old and new and guiding congregations in their design

especially the General Trustees and Church Art and Architecture committee.

Blessing

Bless to us Lord,
our daily routines,
the little kindnesses we do and receive,
the people with whom we interact,
and the paths we travel.
May the Spirit of love and hope
guide all our little steps
in the dance of life itself.

TOWARDS INTIMACY

And the man and his wife were both naked and were not ashamed.

~ Genesis 2:25 NRSV ~

In the story of creation,
Adam and Eve 'knew' each other –
but how well?
For the coupling of flesh alone
can leave the heart unmoved,
and the mind merely diverted
by a moment's pleasure.
Intimacy presumes understanding,
sharing and trusting:
touching places
way beyond the mere physical.

Thank God I can bare my soul
to You, Holy Spirit.
You are my anam cara –
my soul-friend:
I am always in Your company.

Blessed indeed are we
who find a soul-mate –
in partner, or parent, or child,
or simply in a trusted friend.
Lonely indeed are those
who do not find their anam cara
in another.

Yet You urge us on:
risk, love, trust –
life is a journey towards intimacy!

Creator God,
You know me intimately.
I kneel, naked before You
and You clothe me in grace.
Thank You for those to whom I am closest.
Help me to take myself as soul friend too.

Readings

Prayer Activity

Close relationships are part of God's will for humanity imaged in the relationship of Father, Son and Holy Spirit. Sometimes the smallest gesture can be intimate – a hand on the shoulder, a kiss on the top of the head, even a knowing smile. Silence, too, can be intimate when we simply rest in the presence of another. In your own life, what are or have been your most intimate moments with God?

Prayer for the Church

Those who help us to understand the ways of God, our Bibles and to be consistent in the way we present credible Christianity. Theologians, apologists and Christian writers

especially 'Why Believe', Worship and Doctrine Taskgroup.

Blessing

> May the divine spark within You,
> the company of Jesus
> and the love of God
> hold you in intimate fellowship
> until the time comes
> for your final communion.

PROMISED LAND

Then the Lord said to Moses, 'This is the land that I promised Abraham, Isaac and Jacob I would give to their descendants. I have let you see it, but I will not let you go there.'

~ Deuteronomy 34:4 ~

At key moments in our lives, Lord,
we stand on the brink.

All that has gone before,
the road travelled, lies behind
and the view in front of us
seems vast and overwhelming.

Like Moses, we stand today for a moment –
neither here nor there,
breathing in, taking in
the vision, the promise.
It is an awesome, amazing moment,
a faithful glimpse of your plan, trusted and rejoiced in.

But down from the mount, back to the road,
away from the stretching view,
the future seems uncertain, insecure, confusing;
looking back creates longing and loss;
moving forward brings fear, anxiety and crisis of confidence.

So guide us, God, as we travel,
strengthen us on the way,
comfort us in our reflections,
give us again the moments that count
and mean so much,
for you are with us – as promised.

Readings

John 14:1–7   *Jesus, the way*
Psalm 119:145–9   *Meditating on promises*
Hebrews 8:3–6   *Promises of better things*

Prayer Activity

Take some time to think of your church history or even family history. Who was it who passed on to you the teachings of Jesus? Who told you about God? Remember now those who have gone before us who gave their lives to truth and service. What did they work for in the church and society? Did they live to see these things come about? What would they be encouraged to see happening today? Meditate on the thoughts you have around these questions.

Prayer for the Church

That the Good News may be told and read in all languages, and responded positively to. That newspaper editors and news broadcasters might promote truth

especially those we know personally, or because of celebrity, who are involved with the reporting of news through local and national media. Pray also for the work of Bible Societies, making known the Word of God in scripture.

Blessing

Guide me, O thou great Jehovah,
Pilgrim through this barren land;
I am weak, but thou art mighty;
Hold me with thy powerful hand.

CH4 167

RESURRECTION JOURNEY

Jesus said to them 'Come and have breakfast.'

~ John 21:12 ~

Emergency situations, life-changing revelations,
Adrenalin pumping, panic stricken, drama that overwhelms –
Happy are those who experience the ordinary.

Days that blur together, food that has no taste or effect,
Noises and smells and thoughts of never being home again –
Happy are those who get out of hospital.

Memories of what once was, photographs and songs that stir,
Tears and pangs and waves of what will never be again –
Happy are those who find new relationships.

Convinced by a need, dependent on a substance,
Spiralling down, justifying actions, risking all –
Happy are those who do not want.

Everything changed, no way forward,
Hitting rock bottom, nothing to lose, no going back –
Happy are those who know their need of God.

Resurrection God,
May all who are weak and weary, desperate and exhausted,
Know the hope and transforming power of your love
Whatever hell they go through.
May they see a new morning
like your broken disciples
who sat in your presence and ate.   AMEN.

Readings

John 20:1–10   *The resurrection of Jesus*
John 21:1–14   *Resurrection breakfast*
Matthew 5:1–12   *Happy are those ...*

Prayer Activity

Call to mind someone from the news, your community, family or circle of friends who has been through an overwhelming circumstance. Notice how they have coped, how far they have come – what does their journey teach you?

Prayer for the Church

Those who assist us to take our place in, and be enriched by, the experience and witness of the Christian Church where we are at this present time

especially those who brought us to faith, those who pray for us regularly and those with whom we share our faith daily.

Blessing

Breathe on me, Breath of God;
Fill me with life anew,
That I may love the way you love,
And do what you would do.

CH4 595

Serving Overseas with the Church of Scotland

with their families (to be added to the Prayer for the Church for each day)

Day 1	MALAWI: Helen Scott
Day 2	MALAWI: David and Rebecca Morton
Day 3	ZAMBIA: Jenny Featherstone
Day 4	ZAMBIA: Keith and Ida Waddell
Day 5	BAHAMAS: Scott and Anita Kirkland
Day 6	BAHAMAS: John and Carol Macleod
Day 7	TRINIDAD: Garwell and Claudette Bacchas
Day 8	BANGLADESH: David and Sarah Hall
Day 9	BANGLADESH: James and Linda Pender
Day 10	PAKISTAN: Susan Clark
Day 11	ISRAEL and PALESTINE: Antony and Darya Short
Day 12	ISRAEL and PALESTINE: James and Nicola Laing
Day 13	ISRAEL and PALESTINE: George and Margaret Shand
Day 14	ISRAEL and PALESTINE: Ian Alexander
Day 15	ISRAEL and PALESTINE: Jimmy Maxwell
Day 16	ISRAEL and PALESTINE: Colin Johnston
Day 17	LAOS: Tony and Katherine Paton (Mission Associates)
Day 18	BELGIUM: Andrew and Julie Gardner
Day 19	BERMUDA: Barry and Hilda Dunsmore
Day 20	FRANCE: Alan and Lucie Miller
Day 21	GERMANY: Jimmy and Heike Brown
Day 22	GERMANY: Rhona Dunphy
Day 23	HUNGARY: Aaron and Edit Stevens
Day 24	ITALY: William McCulloch
Day 25	MALTA: Doug and Lesley McRoberts
Day 26	THE NETHERLANDS: Robert and Lesley Ann Calvert
Day 27	THE NETHERLANDS: John and Gillian Cowie
Day 28	SRI LANKA: John and Patricia Purves
Day 29	SWITZERLAND: Ian and Roberta Manson
Day 30	Faithshare visitors to Scotland
Day 31	KEN ROSS and the staff at World Mission Council

Acknowledgements

Scriptural quotations, unless otherwise stated, are from the *New Revised Standard Version*, © 1989 Division of Christian Education of the National Council of the Churches of Christ in the United States of America, published by Oxford University Press.

Pray Now 2010 was prepared by members of the Pray Now Group: Gayle Taylor, Carol Ford, Fiona Fidgin, Ewan Kelly, Tina Kemp and Owain Jones.

For further information about *Pray Now* and other publications from the Office for Worship and Doctrine, contact:

> Office for Worship and Doctrine
> Mission and Discipleship Council
> Church of Scotland
> 121 George Street
> Edinburgh EH2 4YN
> Tel: 0131 225 5722 ext. 359
> Fax: 0131 220 3113
> e-mail: wordoc@cofscotland.org.uk

We gratefully acknowledge Gayle Taylor and Chris Cruickshank for their kind permission to reproduce the pictures used in this book.